FOR THE RECORD

FOR THE RECORD

RARITIES, CLASSICS AND BOOTLEGS

Includes out takes and bonus track

ROSS DONLON

RECENT
WORK
PRESS

For the record
Recent Work Press
Canberra, Australia

Copyright © Ross Donlon, 2021

ISBN: 9780648936787 (paperback)

Cover image: the author taken by Brendan Bonsack, at *La Mamma,* Melbourne.
Reproduced with permisssion.
Cover design: Rachael Wenona Guy & Recent Work Press
Set by Recent Work Press

recentworkpress.com

SS

For Ron Pretty

Contents

RARITIES

August   *(0.31)*   3
The Temple   *(0.35)*   4
Poem in December   *(0.52)*   5

PRELUDE

Death in Rome   *(2.21)*   9

CLASSICS

The Bread Horse   *(1.42)*   13
Cicadas   *(1.09)*   14
A boy among men,   *(1.10)*   15
Storm Water   *(1.58)*   16
Budgies   *(0.46)*   18
Mrs Wong   *(1.82)*   19
Questions for the Dead   *(2.39)*   20
Mothers' Day   *(1.29)*   22
Engine Driver   *(2.29)*   23
Watching with Nan   *(0.57)*   24
At Haberfield Demonstration School   *(1.30)*   25
Contact 1942   *(0.52)*   26
Bill 1946   *(1.01)*   27
Trawling in the Arctic   *(1.25)*   28
Evidence   *(0.16)*   29
The Blue Dressing Gown   *(0.58)*   30
By Parramatta River I Lay Down   *(1.22)*   31
The Manly Boys   *(0.53)*   32
The Last Day   *(1.19)*   33
On the Road   *(1.49)*   34
The Bridge   *(1.02)*   36
The Boy and the Suitcase   *(2.03)*   37
Separation   *(0.50)*   38
the good father and his daughter kiss   *(0.35)*   39
Midsummer night   *(2.08)*   40
If Further Evidence Were Needed   *(2.05)*   42
Glass Air   *(1.23)*   43

Shh *(0.53)* 44

with her *(1.13)* 45

Man and Moisturiser *(1.19)* 46

Night Train *(1.02)* 47

Oya Monatharam Lassanada *(1.05)* 48

Old Rakes *(1.18)* 50

Some Reasons to Have a T.U.R.P *(2.56)* 51

Stepping Stones *(1.40)* 53

A Critique—'This is Just to Say' *(0.21)* 55

Gold *(2.40)* 56

Eating Chips with Jane Austen *(3.42)* 57

In Praise of Washing *(0.52)* 59

Bio *(1.20)* 60

BOOTLEGS

My Ship *(1.59)* 63

Continental Drift *(0.41)* 64

Bread *(1.17*) 65

Butter *(1.35)* 66

Knife *(1.26)* 67

The Horses *(0.54)* 68

origin of the species *(0.47)* 69

Feathers *(1.10)* 70

Winter Poem *(0.59)* 71

Body Corporate *(1.08)* 72

Piano Tuner *(1.53)* 73

Mending Boots *(0.51)* 75

Loving Pop *(1.27)* 76

After *(1.56)* 77

Road Kill *(1.11)* 78

All or Nothing *(2.15)* 79

Warren Mathews *(1.19)* 81

Portrait of a Refugee *(5.45)* 82

Refuge / Refugee *(0.52)* 85

In an Antique Land *(1.05)* 86

The First One *(1.10)* 87

After the Election—On Rye Pier *(0.47)* 88

Sunblock *(0.50)* 89

Lemonicious* *(1.02)* 90

Being Puggle *(1.28)* 91

Vampire *(0.40)*   92

Rose *(0.41)*   93

Giant Steps *(1.41)*   94

Walking on Green Cheese *(1.11)*   95

In Your Wake *(1.18)*   96

The Man with a Bucket *(1.05)*   97

The Metaphor-Boat *(2.31)*   98

The Rain in Garana *(1.19)*   99

To the Viewer *(1.03)*   100

Reconciliation *(1.07)*   101

Lady from the Lake *(0.47)*   102

Let's Call This *(1.14)*   103

Geraniums *(1.38)*   104

The Sex *(0.51)*   105

Titanic *(0.57)*   106

(On) About Suffering *(1.11)*   107

the origin of the poem *(0.27)*   108

Netball in Newlyn *(0.57)*   109

After Yorick *(0.33)*   110

At the Poetry Reading *(1.20)*   111

At the (Much Wenlock) Poetry Festival *(1.12)*   112

OUT TAKES

Fables for Our Time 1: The Sheep and the Asteroid *(1.42)*   115

Fables for Our Time 2 : The Trials of Sheep Dog *(2.10)*   116

Fables for Our Time 3: Sammy the Sheep *(1.32)*   117

BONUS TRACK

After the Fall *(1.35)*   121

Afterword   122

RARITIES

August

I looked from my window
and saw the stains of catherine wheels
on the dark wood
and fences shuttered split in tinned-in yards.
Lost in a soft, grey sun
the brown still-life world
rushed down and hushed the turning leaves
until they slept.
                    The lily stalked green
and grew upright
and knew the circle wrought the change
that burnt the leavers around the garden.

The Bulletin, May 22, 1965

The Temple

If you look from the temple
across to the fields where the sun shatters the sight
and the grain breaks in a white light you will know
you may not lose yourself.

I can feel my hand,
its pallor,
its emptiness is the loss of life,
life lost while my eyes have stared into the darkness.

Come,
touch the softness struck in sheets.
The road has left and falling,
I do not know why the evening should ever leave us.

The Bulletin, July 10, 1965

Poem in December

For Glenn Orbell

The days walked over,
their long gowns plucking
at motionless fingers
and although my hands, lifted
sometimes sheltered my sight
at what might have been, perhaps,
a day's life,
I know, today I know,
I can sense my deathlessness.

The moments in which I am content
are those which are not sought for.
The sharp, sour musk of mid-morning
is life, albeit rotting,
and I find in the dusk's positivity
a comfort, a ridiculous comfort.

On this boat
there is much time to think.
Wild, dappled spots
stream out in the wake
like petals thrown behind me.

I wish it were not so.

The Bulletin, April 6, 1966

PRELUDE

Death in Rome

 I saw Death
                in a square in Rome,
quite near the Vatican in fact.
It was too hot for Death,
                nearly 40° Centigrade
and the plaza swarming with passers-by,
the scammers, scammed and the damned,
moving bee-like stall to stall, stopping to dip
into a pocket, purse then gelato.

Poor Death,
in her black hoodie,
black jeans and leather boots
with the silver straps attached,
white makeup glistening buds of sweat,
half-moon eye shadow below two black suns,
she was more like Death-Warmed-Up than Death.

Death needed the coffin
she climbed on
to get her head above the ignorant crowd,
legs braced as though trying to stay afloat,
leaning a bony arm on her scythe,
the black tape fluttering from its blade.

Death had a black cape
spread before her
but I was too far away (I was avoiding Death)
to see whether tribute was forthcoming.
Customers seemed distracted by being alive.
Still, she was patient, looking blankly into the future,
sitting down now and then to smoke on the coffin,
elbows on knees, shoulders hunched.

Death saw me
during one of these smokos.
I was cruising on the edge of the cosmos, pretending
invisibility, even invincibility. But up looked Death
and stared straight at me with a smile of recognition.

Death might be like this, I thought,
a sudden sense of looking into life's last black hole,
outer space becoming inner space without the star trek,
then the familiarity of going home.

I nearly spoke to Death then
but being shy by nature, superstitious, anxious,
and not having Latin (or Italian) and wondering
anyway how an ordinary man can help Death,
I hurried to St Peter's for some beads I had to buy,
some ceilings I had to see, some pomp and pain I had to witness,
before I died.

CLASSICS

The Bread Horse

the glory of his nostrils is terrible
Job. 39.20

The bread cart is parked outside a Glebe delicatessen
owned by the Nackens, who I will never see again.
My grandmother works for them this one day,
and I must play on the sawdust floor
under their red faces, white aprons
and the curtain of sausages.

Heat from the bread cart and horse droppings
make sweet street perfume. Tram lines
shimmer between weaving cars and lorries,
and the footpath will be my first stage performance
since I must perform the Feeding Trick with an apple,
fingers straight as instructed, *unless you want to lose them*.
Lifted to the horse's nostrils, orange teeth,
clanking, metal mouth and head as big as me,
I have a presentiment of Apocalypse,
but his whiskery lips clean up both core and chunks,
and his leather tongue soothes my fingers.
I hear the jingle of harness as a signal to look -
at twitching ears, a chestnut fringe cut straight,
splash of milk spilt on a forehead,
our reflections in each other's eyes.
Then his hooves wake, shuffle, clop away,
reins snapping his back as the wheels clatter.
The memory hovers like kindness,
like the comfort of hot bread,
years after traffic covers his tracks.

Cicadas

They came to us from far away,
their older selves left
like suitcases at the door.
We crushed them as we walked to school
or crunched the silver shells to crystal.

When summer broke above our small backyards
and hot winds woke the neighbour's trees
we caught cicadas clinging to the leaves
shook them til they screamed
stripped the fairy wings
(tiny stained glass windows fluttering down)
then squeezed until they pissed inside our fists.

Once we kept some in a cage
feeding them with boredom,
watching as they tried to understand
the metal floor and plastic swing
but found them still in the morning on their backs
as though they'd crashed while racing in the dark
feelers gesturing,
bodies posed for photographs.

We went off to explore the choko vines
and trails of rainbows left behind by snails,
our petal eyes wide open,
faces pushed like feelers into leaves
(and the mystery of chokos)
still learning how to see.

A boy among men,

squashed in the truck cabin
hearing their steering wheel talk
turn to Saturday afternoon
while others hang on to the back
of the flatbed swaying on chains.

At Brookvale Oval the crowd swirls
with smoke and swearing
and the sweet smell of beer and the shouting
is laughing or angry when the whistle scores
or players lunge at the fence.

A boy between legs and coats
feels small as the ball
sees patterns of colour running away
the kicked leather grunts
black and white guernseys mix with maroon
then a dull roar at the end
and words stubbed out
quietly as cigarettes.

After shadows cover the sunshine of grass
men meet in half-light behind the grandstand
to sort out the fight that began in the crowd.
Toilet walls thud with blood but somehow
it ends with a handshake.
Going home half drugged from sun and soft drink
the boy sees gods on the back of the flatbed
hardly hanging onto their chains
then dinner of baked leg of lamb, apple pie
and women, waiting.

Storm Water

We found it on a summer ride,
sliding down the cambered side

barefoot, our scooters parked
in the shade like getaway cars.

The town's concrete scar
ran behind sheds and yards,

water rippling down its spine
like gold in holiday sunshine.

Nearby, blocks of factory walls,
locked gates and chained doors

were easy for boys to slip through
on weekends. We wandered into

yards, canteens, offices and sheds,
finding kitchens, toilets, a bed

and peeling posters of beach girls
who grinned over their shoulders.

Parents weren't told, so couldn't warn,
how rain is channelled after a storm

and the boy-sized drain so near home
longed for explorers. Ant had stones

for protection, so our torches roamed walls
as we galloped, splashed and called.

The dark made us hoot like ghost trains.
There were no skeletons, but we found remains

where soft shadows rustled before us
and echoes answered. Rats? Vampire bats?

Each second was a fairground for the senses,
a lifetime journey under backyard fences.

There were steps to a manhole. We craned
like gophers in a Loony Tunes cartoon

and saw a concrete yard swathed in blood
where a man washed gore from butcher's tubs

into the gutter. We thrilled with fright
running like victims to the distant light

that finally became the canal's wide brim.
Four heroes entered an empty stadium.

And no one was hurt, no one died,
carried away on a nightmare tide,

but I think of our luck, fifty years on,
that dark rollercoaster ride to oblivion

we missed, never hearing the sound
of Death coming for us underground.

Budgies

They taught me to be tender, claws
clutching my fingers like small children
holding on as we might cross the road.
And when storms crashed or a spreadeagled cat
slammed them back and forth in the dark
I was afraid for them, playmates of an only child.

I gave them love, names, and histories,
learned about life and death—for some did die,
cold as cuttlefish on the sandy floor
so their leaving was hard to understand.

When the door on the cage banged open
in a southerly gale, their rush to escape
seemed disloyal. They blew away, shrilling
into the waiting maw of an open sky.

Mrs Wong

Ashfield Grocer circa. 1950

He runs to her shop, scene
from his Saturday movie matinee -
Hong Kong. Tangiers. Mandalay.

Enter a boy with a message.
Enter Mrs Wong doorway
hand draped in clicking glass.

She floats to him, blue shape
quiet in the sound of slippers,
beads' applause in her wake,

eyes not seeing but knowing
through razor lids, *The boy*
is here, near the lolly jars

with his list for vegetables.
He raises the paper scrap
to an idol in turquoise

who packs the few goods
as though they are crystal,
parchment hands blue with maps.

No words, unless those heard
at the end of a long journey.
No carrot today.

She nods goodbye,
a spearmint leaf sparkling
in his hand like jade.
.

Questions for the Dead

For Margaret Phelps

By night, your Necropolis could be a city skyline -
neighbours on rooftops with t.v. antennas.

By day, crucifixes chess piece their way
through a thousand flocks of angels

perched on marble or outside mausoleums
waiting the world to end or one to wake.

There's disorientation being lone searcher
in a city of dead and gridlocked streets.

Inside the shrubs and patchwork plan
a million souls lie ready and waiting,

like vehicles left in a stadium car park,
motors running until maps arrive.

Religions intertwine like overlapping galaxies,
signs point uncertainly to chapels and shrines

so it's understandable that finding you
and Kathleen, your stillborn grandchild,

would be difficult, the helpful numbers
well hidden behind trees and uncut grass.

Our time provides no grave goods
to comfort either side of eternity,

no clues as to who you were, a life
with bookends but few books -

a deathbed drenched by *The Change*
is the only story that made it here.

Words wear fast even with a headstone's gravity.
Your site turns out wordless, looking straight up

into the questions each day has to offer
and at night, the cartography of stars.

Mothers' Day

For Margaret Phelps and Mary Veronica Lang

After the cups of tea and gifts of slippers
we always went to Rookwood Cemetery -

walk train walk again in swimming heat,
me bobbing behind your trailing hand.

To a small boy, your mother's grave
alongside her stillborn grandchild

looked like a door or pebbled floor,
somewhere to rest after the long trip

safe inside the concrete arms, away
from buffalo grass, the nip of prickles.

No need to caution me about respect.
You knelt on newspaper and looked hard

at what a year had left. Life doesn't respect
Death - the plastic dome of flowers cracked.

You had the hand shears and garden fork
to hedge grass back. I yanked at runners.

Both graves looked better for the work,
white crysanths we bought from a stall

glittering in jars on the heart of the grave -
posies of bright suns awake in the glass.

Later, there was something to eat and drink
in one of the nearby hive shaped rotundas.

Lattice walls patterned us, blurring light
and shade, you quiet now with memory,

your mother out of the grave's clean door,
joining us in the half light, sipping tea.

Engine Driver

O Grandpa was a steam train man,
I watched him pass in a cinder shower.
All trains rocked to his blunt, hard name,
Jack Strang, strength. Jack Strang, power.

Shell shocked eyes in a war torn face,
hob nail boots and soldier's walk,
rage no passing year erased
for a family too afraid to talk.

O trains pass boys like rivers of dreams
when you watch for a face in a cabin of fire
but carriages joined with elephants' tails
rattled down tracks with no goodbye.

Up at crack, sun on his back
flint heeled boots sparked a lightning path
but then one day he went to the pack;
a coal black cough cut his life in half.

Work all done he took to his bed,
blankets became his gullies and hills,
shouting the names of wounded and killed,
fighting the war until he was dead.

Watching with Nan

For my grandmother, Mary Veronica Lang

She was so used to being good
that when Parkinson discovered her,
like an explorer spoiling all he found,
she was easy to institutionalise,
to be put into bed and left there.
In a chrysalis of hairnet and sheets
Nan peeked a hook nose from beneath,
like Judy after Punch was done
(but actually, it was a horse
which had obliged with a kick
when she jumped a fence to tease it.)
In our small upstairs flat
she sang between the stove and sink
dancing me on slippertoes. Music Hall.
Eddie Cantor. Al Johnson.
Pop let her go to work
running dance classes in Newtown.
She and I watched cars race down
Bland Street, counting and marvelling
while I learned numbers and colours
and how everything goes away.

At Haberfield Demonstration School

I was with the boys in our group
at the meeting place, a peppercorn tree,
eating lunch inside the shadow.
The peppercorns' bright, spicy scent
remains in memory,
the way it stays on fingers with the stain.

Soon I would be ready for the Big School,
separated from the girls' asphalt playground
of rectangles, circles and squares.
The boys played war
up and down a sloping paddock
beyond the classroom.
We heard their cries a continent away.

Suddenly the talk turned to fathers
and what they *did*.
As turns edged around the circle like a clock
I discovered that I could not speak.
what was it that I could not say?

The bell saved me as I was falling.
A huge part of who I thought I was
had avalanched, as if a shelf
had fallen from a mountain.

I was an obedient child
but I ran home from school to my Nan,
family skittled by a missing pin.

We sat on her bed and looked at photographs
and a face the size of a fingernail. Bill.
From the war.
She fanned the pictures out like playing cards.
It was a summer afternoon.
The bedroom's lace curtains glowed in tiny squares
and a wind blew the sweet scent
from Peak Frean's biscuit factory
while the bitumen noise of cars rushed down our street.

Contact 1942

In trying to tell me, words stop
as shoulders and hands
attempt to remake him—
her face recalling the shock,
as though she'd turned a corner, opened a gift,
opened her eyes, or had them opened
by something amazing.

In over sixty years
I have no experience of her
to prepare for how she is now.
Not like the pleasure I've seen
as she holds a grandchild, finishes a jumper,
or demonstrates, at eighty-five,
her mastery of technology—
no reference for this moment
as she tries again to explain,
as though it was a kind of birth,
something I'll never understand.

Now, she almost groans with the memory of it.
It was, she says, *Oh*,
and tries to shape the waterfall of air in front of her
into a man.

Bill 1946

From a photograph in Louisville, Kentucky, 1946

A year of peace has yet to make him a civilian.
Despite the pressed suit, collar and tie,
ex-serviceman's badge gleaming
like a talisman on his lapel,
he still has war in his backbone.
Hands clasped behind him
try to be at ease.

His face juts for the camera,
jaw set, shoulders braced,
almost a forties' comic book character.
Fearless Fosdick, Dock Tracey, Joe Palooka
are all sure he's gonna make it.

He is packed for 'Frisco.
Bound for Sydney, Aussieland.
Hair oiled and combed
so hard you can see his scalp.
Standing beside his niece and nephew.
dark tower at the backyard going away,
the lines of weatherboard on his parents' house
stretch behind him to a vanishing point.

Trawling in the Arctic

Sometimes we trawled with the midnight sun
a gold bullet hole in the horizon,
sometimes in sleet, the cod masked in ice.
Once we trawled in the tail of a cyclone,
the stern under wash, sea slashed
black and white into spray.

You got to the galley by counting waves,
Sliding and crashing across the deck,
and I thought of the seafarer
in the Old English poem,
a peat bog man, offshore in a storm,
caught by cold, raw wind wracking,
ice biting, as he hunted for home.

Still young, I watched a coast creep by
While the ship rode waves like a surfer,
Then rucked my oilskin around my ears
and ran, regardless of wind, spray
and counting.
          At such times, looking out
from my own tightrope, I trawl for my father
in a 'Frisco dive, rain ramming, his walk home wet
lit only by neon, and nobody there.

I reflect, like someone watching the sea,
how he waited for ships in the Ferry Hotel,
the irony tolling across the Pacific
to a war wife and son in Sydney,
one barely known, one never seen
as he buffeted life towards death.

Evidence

Compared to a day
it's a minute or two

if an hourglass
a few grains that slipped through

a slip of light on a sundial
before lightning struck

out the name
I bear from you.

The Blue Dressing Gown

It hung in my boy's wardrobe,
an army regulation item
no one could throw out.

And it would be hard, wouldn't it
to discard the only thing left
in something like the shape of him.

It hung on a wire hanger,
skeleton of his shoulder
cutting across collar bone,

the drape of it swinging side to side
if nudged into a shy dance
or asked up by a breeze.

I used to wear it, with no sense
of feeling weird or spooky,
alternating with a practical flannel,

yet at night sometimes woke
frightened by its doorway shadow,
a man hanging on the moon's hook.

I never realised I'd outgrown him,
walking tall through one summer
while his shoulders rode my back.

The tassels swung like incense
as I walked in his shape
trying to sense the being inside him.

By Parramatta River I Lay Down

Mrs P. Mrs A. Mrs R. R. A!
Mrs M. Mrs A. Mrs T. T. A!
chant the Westmead girl cousins
on the muddy banks of the Parra River in Parramatta Park.
Everything is Parramatta.
The lesson is how to spell 'Parramatta'.
to the too easily-teased city coz
in his going-out outfit, not fit for the Parra.

Half-boys, they swing river ropes being both Tarzan & Jane,
strew their bodies in the sun like a puzzle,
swim crocodiles under reeds, clap arm-jaws,
aim sharks at the Ashfield statue stuck to his ankles.

The afternoon disrobes in sequins,
river invading him with probable snakes,
quicksands, snags, rips & curtains of weeping willow
which close on childhood & open on adolescence.
The bookish cousin
feels pages turning on the act so fast
his eyes blur with the speed of the rapids projecting time
until he emerges, primeval, lays down in the mud,
exhausted & newly crawled out specimen of evolution,
girl-watched & watching, child-skin washed off in
the Parramatta River.

The Manly Boys

They dived for coins where the ferry docked,
slotting loose change beneath their tongues,
stopping us as we arrived for the day,
white faced and fresh from the suburbs.

Lolling in the water, *the Manly Boys*,
eye whites upraised and cheeks full,
watched a tossed bob sparkle and flicker,
then enter the water in a flash of light
before they ducked under faster than the coin
spangled and sashayed, until fingers slipped silver
quick as a doubloon, inside pirate lips.

From the other side of the sea's glass,
they were a boy I could never be,
they a man-boy, seal-like, sea being
me a child on leave from a suburb,
longing either to be that boy,
or else the coin held tight in his mouth.

The Last Day

Form 5 Photograph Fort Street Boys' High School, Sydney. 1962

Here we are (or were) on the school steps.
Our prefects, seated in front with the principal,
a set of solid sphinxes, with fists parked on knees,
seem older than us who stand behind them,
less assured of future work, degrees and girls.
Academic rank and promise also decline
as rows climb steps until bottom is top.
Haloes above front row boys also fade with altitude
and attitude, slip at rakish angles over smirks and smiles,
morph into question marks on clowns and fools,
and those whose third eye is a headache for now.
Higher still, my mates lean or slouch in half-uniform
and somewhere in the shade of the last sun
I've hidden in the shadow of a boy in front.
Yet as the phalanx of Fortians, Class of Sixty-Two,
freeze like adults for the last shot, I change my mind
(as might be expected) to peek out half-face,
one of the dreamy clueless; no prospects, no idea, poet.

On the Road

One for the El Rocco

It's a grainy strip of memory in black and white,
King's Cross lights flashing on and off upstairs,

us just out of school at the edge of the sixties
with one hot shot at being a beatnik in Sydney.

Joan Baez was there. Four of her made instant coffee
and burnt raisin toast downstairs at the *El Rocco*.

We smoked more than we breathed, lighting
up a new Peter Stuyvesant *international passport*

to smoking pleasure from the ash of the last,
teenage phoenixes, hoping inhalation meant

European women in white slacks, barely
buttoned shirts or bikinis banned in Australia.

We knew to tap a matchbox to the beat
sip instant coffee beneath our sunglasses,

clap after solos, and nod to the musos
as if we knew them and what they were doing.

I'd read *On the Road*, been drunk and beat,
pub crawled from the Quay up George Street

to the Cross, drinking alcohol alphabetically
or by colour following the rainbow's spectrum.

Waves of harder drugs were forming
but we'd gone before they broke and stars started

to fall apart onstage. I entered another looking glass,
saw tablets marked, *Travel and Sex—Take for Five Years*.

By the time I climbed out, still hung over but older,
disco balls had incinerated duffle coats and cords.

Nostalgic for old times, I checked the goods trains
piling through Ashfield, heading west in the dark

but gave up wondering how to get on and off them
and what might have happened if I'd ended up in Parkes.

The Bridge

During the Great Depression, construction
of the pylons of Sydney Harbour Bridge
displaced eight hundred families.
No compensation for the Great Scattering
at a time when the poor went shoeless
under canvas and corrugated iron.

Workers poured white hot ingots on site
as spans grew skywards from expendable men.
Sixteen died. Six fell, clothes streaming from them
into the hard glass of Sydney Harbour -
the shock welded boots to their dead feet.
Spans were edging closer then,
almost like outstretched arms,
but too late to prevent men dropping
through a postcard to Eternity.

Eighty years on, tourists look down and out
through viewfinders. They pay well
to walk over the arch in bright overalls,
sliding in chains along the safety rails.
Not even a Southerly Buster
can blow them away.

The Boy and the Suitcase

A suitcase was known to a small boy. It was a tartan patterned suitcase, made in China, manufactured in a large factory that made backpacks, bags and the like. A production line of hundreds of workers worked in the factory and had done so for years. I think there may even be a museum somewhere whose purpose is to display the history of bags, packs and suitcases with their various designs and uses.

The tartan suit case was unusual in that it lived in two homes. In one house it was kept in a dark wardrobe with safe, folded clothes. In the other house it stayed on the floor between noises in the kitchen and bedroom - some muted, some loud. There were times of sudden floods of light.

Every month the suitcase travelled between the two houses by car. When it was time to visit, neat sets of clothes and toys were packed and the suitcase would travel in the car with the boy.

On the last visit there were hours of calm, then a sudden explosion of sound and silence.

A day passed. The lid was opened with a burst of light and crying, and the boy was folded like clothes into the suitcase, after which it was closed, locked and carried to a car.

It will not be the first time a suitcase has been placed in water to drown. It may not be the first time a small boy has been pressed into a suitcase, to play or be punished. It may not be the first time a tartan suitcase of moderate size has risen to the surface of a suburban lake and been opened to find a small boy inside.

But it always seems as though it is the first time.

Then, as old rites in ancient Egypt or the peat bogs of Denmark, the case will be opened and a body raised to the small sun watching from the sky like a host.

Separation

Raised by his hand into the sky at dusk
his flock dissolves above the small backyard.
He watches for them from the shrubs and dust,
a family breaking like a deck of cards.

Their calm, grey wings and simple nodding heads
become wind waves that ripple on the sun,
a soaring instinct in the birds who spread
beyond the cage the suburb has become.

You feel the weight as they pull overhead,
watching from inside the rented flat
and wonder if the will that holds the thread
is strong enough to make your own come back.

Next door the sound of sudden flight subsides.
Your neighbour's children tumble from the sky.

the good father and
his daughter kiss

they lean towards each other
as safe from folding as a pyramid
yet fragile as the baby fist
she shook aloft like lightning
when he was the boat she sailed in
harbour to safe harbour
now he makes sure hips don't touch
and hands are placed on shoulders just so
and lips kiss one centimetre left of lips
then she turns
and flows into her mother
like a river

Midsummer night

For Ingeborg Kroll

In Álvik the festival of Midsummer Night is at eight o'clock
but there's a sense of displacement or disorientation.
We tourists want it to be midnight,
expectation of fantasy over a screen of fact,
but it's still broad daylight on an overcast day.
Clouds like fallen towers edge along the fjord,
fine films of rain keep the scene shifting,
new images drift over the wooden reels piled like an altar,
a foreshore pyre billows next to the town's fire truck,
a fireman in protective gear slews fuel on the flames.

We expected other signs across the water,
other torches along the picturesque rim,
other symbols as the night came on,
perhaps a romance of paganism,
primal fire before the light of Christianity,
but the water only smoked with rain.

Enough witches were burned in Christian Norway,
some in Bergen, eighteen once up north in Vardø
to warrant two monuments. Both are in the guides.
All were women condemned by strange weather,
neighbours' hysteria and the encouragement of torture.
Being Norway, there's an architect designed
memorial in Vardø. The illusion of an empty chair
is consumed by flames inside a glass space,
as though regret for what happened in 1621
must be never ending, the constant, almost animate fire
more awful, more alive, than stone.

In Vardø only Ingeborg Kroll refused to confess
to flying, drowning sailors or having a tour of hell
before her body gave up to white hot cuts
and her chest burned with sulphur.
Buried on an island opposite the gallows
the shape stretches like another judgment.

In Ålvik children gather in the roped front row
sitting cross legged, themselves tiny idols
who look up and down from the cameras
which they nurse and touch as tenderly as manikins.

Most settle to watch the digital version
once removed from reality,
able to edit and save the furnace of wheels on fire.
Eventually the reels begin to topple
and roll into themselves.
Their round faces look up burning
before rows of screens, a smiling crowd,
and one thousand years of shadows
while small boys, as ever, cry,

More diesel. More diesel.

If Further Evidence Were Needed

'Waves of invaders' is a gentle sounding phrase
for what happens when killing becomes tidal.
Western Romania knew centuries of invasion
until in an act displaying some attempt at finality,
Austro-Hungarians levelled the capital, Tmişoara.
They left just the fortress of King Robert Charles of Anjou
as a marker or playing counter on the swampy crossroads.
Then they built an outpost or memory of Vienna.
A canal cured the swamp. City planners mapped
millimetre perfect squares and streets in the wake
of the Ottoman retreat, like boys saying, *So there.*
Three centuries later in a park near the centre,
I scan a map looking for wordslips of history,
shards of language, half-lost names, any accidental
echo of those otherwise consumed or swept away.
Lines radiate sun-like from the city centre,
bulevard and *strada* celebrate a hand span
of men's names, all drawn from current occupants,
as if reminders are needed as to who they were.
Like proclamations are the *Bulevard of December 16, 1989,*
Bulevard of the Revolution, Bulevard of the Republic,
while *Strada of December 1, 1918,* is a statement
marking both the beginning and end of the world.

Perhaps it's not surprising that the Dacians, Romans
and the hordes of hordes who followed are invisible,
except in faces, daily speech or hints of cuisine.
It's inevitable, I re-consider, that those who lease
a space, name and decorate after their own time.

And far down in a corner, in a new part of town,
close by the university, almost a footnote to the map,
an ironic aside to the evolution of my species
(if any further evidence were needed):
Strada Charles Darwin.

Glass Air

For Susan Mannion

We're chatting in the kitchen at Annaghmakerrig
when there's a sudden flurry outside the window -

a pair of green finches are a whirling burst
of chase mating or tumbling in a birdfight.

But one, the more distracted by excitement,
or deceived that both images of sky are real,

discovers too late that air is suddenly glass,
that nothing has become something hard.

It's a polite bump in our conversation
which we all hear, look up inside to out

to the bird, still and quiet. Someone notices
nothing - no heartbeat or bird's eye quiver.

The partner or rival (partner surely) flits and
flickers but at one remove, as though a second

force keeps the bird away from the window.
One of us asks should we bring it in or wait

for it to wake. But too many minutes go by
as it stares into the garden and only rain

moves its feathers. Later Susan carries it
to a shrub and we sense its tiny heaviness,

chance audience to a mortality play
seen through our own reflections.

Shh

don't kiss me yet
just rest your lips against my mouth
while I taste the faintest touch of you
but breathe me
while our senses scan the past
until we're here
curves and angles resting comfortably
complex lives a perfect fit
then I'll take up your hair
half autumn leaves half sun
and spread the strands upon the pillow
the web of one night's life
then breathe me
while I pin your outstretched arm
to the edge of the world
and breathe me as moonlight spreads
to show the light and dark
we've both come through to be here
and breathe me one last time
and only then please move your mouth
the millimetre more
until it enters mine

with her

and at last she comes to bed
the blue nightie
caught below her knees
and as she bends—like a girl picking flowers—
her breast moves with the movement down
her hair falls to one side

there's a scent of rose and jasmine
and her night crème glows
as she switches off the light
and climbs towards me
while I wait in my singlet and skin
with a useless book and glasses

nearly sixty
yet we slide beneath the sheet
like children slipping beneath the first wave of summer
and it's she who turns first
to fold her hair before it's caught
as I turn to hold her
my palm floating across her back
pausing then stroking again—like soothing something young and wild
shifting her thigh across mine
kissing her lips like a kiss before sleep
when it's really *hello how are you tonight*
and she sighs and says *this is nice*
while our bodies move together like an answer

Man and Moisturiser

My skin is drying—
I'm scaly as a pearly alligator.
But the woman in the pharmacy
is encouraging, even cheerful—
tells me I can use this lotion all over my body.
(Then she pauses, as something occurs to her.)

Back home,
I adopt the pose of every clown or actor
I've seen spread greasepaint over stubble,
Or every woman I've watched
tilt a chin, furrow a tongue,
then roll an eye at a mirror
to better see a spread of skin
and the self inside the self.
And how pleasurable it is,
immersion in a lake of lavender,
how like reversion into childhood's
sun cream, zinc cream, ice cream.

I soothe and spread, fingers breaststroke,
Easing years from the wake I've sailed.
Grinless Easter Island face slips by,
flaws soften and disappear,
my mistakes filled with moisturiser.
I touch and retouch inside the mirror,
until smoother than a Henry Moore man,
past is perfect—no angles, I am an angel again,
wings invisible as my history.

Night Train

As lights go out,
your head knocks against glass,
a dull drum trapping your
reflection.
Outside,
thousands of lives
stream down the line,
arrows and crosses
point warnings
as past becomes future.

Your train heaves
through rushing air,
a kind of time
where time stands still
and only night moves.

We look to the Buffet
Mother for dream
security. Uniforms
and mechanical talk
confirm this is a flight
through space.

We could be sleeping
cadavers in our own body bags,
and this the ante-room
of an afterlife,
but the chrysalis cracks
as we stir, then wake,
surprising each other.

On the outskirts of Sydney.
the moon changes behind trees,
becomes the sun of a new planet.

Pale in the weak morning,
a hot air balloon
hangs still as a gumleaf.
Delicate and tender
it's like being found alive.

Oya Monatharam Lassanada

How Charming You Were (Sinhala)

1.

Late into the next day
I could still taste you

on the tips of my fingers
and in my mouth.

Or was it the food I cooked,
cumin, turmeric, paprika

mixed with your skin's sheen,
the scent of lotus?

Smooth as temple water
you propped a cool head

on one hand, pondering
the prospect of a new lover.

Night dissolved you
into me and out, your clitoris

a silk road towards morning.

2.

I'd never been someone's one-night stand before.

After the heat, the phrase made me think of desert
and me as a distant cactus, green and awkward.

I looked out the open window, a little cold now,
one knee still on the bed, one arm shyly saluting

your Alfa Romeo, as it waved, inscrutable
in its plume of dust, some signal of good bye.

Old Rakes

Old rakes lean in doorways
of garden sheds, elegant, wistful,
comfortable in muted light.

Half-shadowed at night,
they are silver tipped by stars.
The moon tries to draw them out.

Old rakes are smoother than new rakes,
knowing how to handle & be handled,
never on for rough trade.

Their screws are still tight
& the slow pull & push through pretty leaves is easy.
Strokes are varied. Teeth disrobe anything caught.

Other tools are merely that:
oafish shovel & Hadean pitchfork
make hard work of play.

Old rakes enjoy words
like furrow, seed, a good prune, Spring,
love songs by Irving Berlin.

Old rakes creak but never tire,
never retire. Some nights when a certain light strikes
the grin is pure Flynn.

Some Reasons to Have a T.U.R.P

1. To Improve your spelling.

You can improve your spelling and help others by clearly distinguishing between the often confused words, 'prostrate' and 'prostate'. The reply, 'Well no, I am actually having a Trans-Urethal Resection of the Prostate. I will be *prostrate* later by the pool,' clarifies the difference.

2. To Increase Your General Knowledge and Vocabulary

This development will come about as a result of exposure to new medical terms such as, catheter, void, catheter, double void, catheter, bladder spasm. And Catheter.

3. To revitalise Your Expression

Especially in the invention of curses, such as the western, unequivocal, 'May you be transfixed by a thousand catheters' to the eastern, more metaphysical, 'May you never void...'

4. To Reduce Anxiety in Women

A simple badge worn on the lapel, depicting a smiling prostate inside a red circle bisected by a red diagonal line communicates a clear message.

5. To Provide an Insight into Sado Masochism

The procedure of prostate removal provides a chance to experience an S & M Dungeon while in the comparative safety of a hospital. Attention is on the penis and there are procedures by women dressed as nurses. The experience for most men is painful, possibly humiliating—but some may find this otherwise.

6. To Find Consolation in Philosophy

One morning you wake to discover an erection. But find it accompanied by a catheter. The experience is complicated. You want to show and tell but this is not a time for visitors or the nurses' bell. You would like the erection to remain but realise that, for now, it is of no practical use to anyone. Sensations are confused and provide a lively interior dialogue on the relation of pleasure to pain, the rational to the sensual, the mind to the body, the id to the ego; themes often explored in philosophical discourse from Plato to Nietzsche.

7.   *To Alter the Self*

The older self is left behind on a kind of psychic coat hanger at the Nurses' Station, to be collected when you are discharged. For the duration of your stay in hospital you are transformed into your new self, *Darl*, or alternatively, *Love*. The address is nice in an odd way and the perceived affection sometimes makes you want to stay in hospital.

8.   *To Reduce Weight*

The amount of weight loss depends on the size of the formerly enlarged prostate.

Stepping Stones

After the painting, Stepping Stones, *by Rupert Bunny*

A young man, naked, pulls a net through the water.
He is catching fish, braced to the weight,
back and shoulders taut, hips leaning into the catch.
An older woman, heavy with her hard day
and the weight of a sack on her shoulder,
looks down to the upward step
and ignores the naked young man,
not remembering her girlhood.

A young woman, slim, balancing, bent,
bundle on her back, child in front,
weighs the next step.
She does not regard the naked young man
and is not comparing him to the man
she left sleeping in their hut by the river.

The older youth, waiting for the women to pass,
also does not notice the naked young man
toiling naked in the water.
He is not reconsidering
his sexual orientation.

The man ploughing the field concentrates
on heaving oxen and the straight line of furrow,
rather than on the nakedness
of the young fisherman,
fishing naked - and without any clothes on at all—
in the swirling water.
Straining at the net.

Trees, insects and other wildlife
not actually depicted in the painting
similarly complete their day oblivious
to the pull and thrust of the naked young man.
The granite bluff stares pointedly
at some distant aspect, over the heads
of the young fisherman
and the obsessed man and women
who are seemingly intent
on participating in an otherwise meaningless
mythological pageant by Rupert Bunny.

Ray and Judy

After the painting, Ray and Judy, *by John Brack*

Ray and Judy
1,2,3
Swoop across / the old Majestic
1,2,3
Arch their backs / each spine elastic
1,2,3
Crane their necks / like drunken puppets
1,2,3
Hiss foul oaths / if someone stuffs it
1,2,3
Curse the tart / in fleshy scarlet
1,2,3
She bonks the judges / *Bloody Harlot*
1,2,3
Check out Bert / who's nearly past it
1,2,3
His toupee looks like a ferret
1,2,3
Keep a watch / on Frank from Dubbo
1,2,3
Rams contestants / like torpedos
1,2,3
Ray's got something / in his front teeth
1,2,3
Bit of beetroot? / Nope, it's roast beef
1,2,3
Young Breanna's eyes / are popping
1,2,3
He's snagged her skirt / ripped her stocking
1,2,3
If Jude's bra strap snags now / they're cactus
1,2,3
Bang goes all / the weeks of practice
1,2,3
That's the Waltz / end of this lot
1,2,3
Got the big one / in the Foxtrot
1,2,3
1   2   3   4   5

A Critique—'This is Just to Say'

Dear W.C.
the plums that you just ate were meant for me.

Hot or cold I'd meant them for today
to comfort me when you had gone away.

You left me with some Vegemite and toast.
(My application for divorce is in the post).

Gold

The Sydney Olympic Games were amazing, fantastic, unbelievable.
The city looked amazing, fantastic, unbelievable.
Individual performances were amazing, fantastic, unbelievable.
Team spirit was amazing, fantastic, unbelievable.
Organisation was amazing, fantastic, unbelievable.
There were numerous events at numerous venues all involving the human spirit and body being tested to the utmost and all were amazing, fantastic, unbelievable
Competitors ran, swam, jumped, threw, rode or played in team sports and all were amazing, fantastic, unbelievable.
Dawny, Cathy, Betty, Kylie, Thorpie, Olivia and John, Nova, Jumping Jai, Tatiana, the Hockeyroos, the Olyroos, the Channel Seven team, Roy and H.G., Fastso the Fat Arsed Wombat and all of the other little promotional animals, the host of torch bearers, including community workers, and employees of corporations who were part of the sponsorship team, Kevin Gosper and his daughter Sophie and other members of SOCOG and their families were all amazing, fantastic, unbelievable.
Drug abuse and corruption was amazing, fantastic, unbelievable.
The track was a red-brown colour with white stripes in an oval shape. At one end additional white lines joined the shape which made it appear from above like an aboriginal cave painting, representing perhaps a symbol of continuity or a spirit being with long hair.
The pool was a rectangle of blue with straight, black lines running parallel along the length. The swimmers wore black body suits that made them seem like leaves or shadows.
At the conclusion of events, competitors stood, held totems and gifts and received adulation as they raised their arms to the sky.
Sometimes the sky was blue and the sun shone brightly. Sometimes the sky was grey.
There was also cloud, rain and wind.
In some parts of Australia, the sun, cloud, wind and rain were present in places where the Olympic Games did not exist in any sense.
In some high-rise apartment buildings, mid density or outer suburban dwellings or outback rural communities there were those for whom the Olympic Games did not exist in any sense.
Slowly warming, the Earth continued to spin through space during September.
Sometimes it was in darkness, laced only by the moon and stars.
At other times it glowed in its orbit around the sun.
Gold. Gold. Gold.
Amazing. Fantastic. Unbelievable.

Eating Chips with Jane Austen

after Galway Kinnel et al

I often eat a packet of potato chips alone.
I eat them with a can of beer while I watch a cooking program.
This can make the chips taste like the dish
chef is preparing, such as *Crème Caramel* or *Beef Teriyaki*.
I know that it is not good to eat potato chips alone
so sometimes I invite Jane Austen to join me.
Jane is always Jane, the perfect companion:
reserved, tactful, gracious, demure, wise & generous.
I like to observe her in profile as she sits near my air con,
bodice of her gown fluttering from the fan set on Two, a book pleasantly in hand.
She speaks little but her responses to anecdotes regarding the shambles
of my personal life are always expressed in a reassuring & compassionate manner.
It cannot be quite as you say, Sir. Surely it was never so bad as this.
We must look an odd pair, she in her long-sleeved Regency gown buttoned at the wrist,
lace in place, hair drawn up in an understated style, posture both composed & relaxed,
me in my footy shorts & singlet, feet spread on the coffee table.
I know from her half-smile that she registers my attire & the period of time
that separates us, but there is no condescension, no hint that a station has been passed.
She evinces little interest in football, so we do not dwell for too long
on the misfortunes of the Magpies & soft tissue injuries caused by playing on artificial
surfaces.
She is, of course, at her most entertaining & instructive in the matter of social intercourse
& I tell her that in 2016 she would be well paid in a Dear Jane segment on Daytime
Television.
Jane colours a little at this, especially when I indicate that the complications
of sexual relations are now rather more diverse than they were in her day.
Suddenly animated, she says, *Sir, I beg to differ. The issue is always one of compatibility.*
Once, after another keenly felt rejection, I opined that my relationships resembled
nothing so much
as a pair of lonely jocks being tossed about in a cosmic washing machine not even in the
company of detergent.
At this Jane bent rather more closely to her book but I sensed a rebuke when she said she
regretted my *unfortunate use of metaphor.*
I rushed to apologise, blaming the crassness of the age in which I live.
Sir, she replied with wry smile & sparkling eye, *I think you were born into the wrong time.
You are all grace & courtesy & surely the attachment of a fortunate woman will soon be yours.*
Eventually an imposing gentleman comes to collect her, no doubt a hybrid of Mr. Darcy
& Captain Wentworth
He nods briefly in my direction before offering Jane his arm.

Remembering my manners, I offer them each chips & a can of beer.

Darcy-Wentworth appears somewhat taken aback by my hospitality & to tell the truth of the matter

I am by now so covered in crumbs & small pieces of chip that I look rather like a big potato chip myself.

Jane, ever Jane, smiles & declines with sublime courtesy & together they walk through the wall.

In Praise of Washing

I like the sound
of a machine washing,
the pulse and hum,
the snoring slosh,
the butterfly murmurs
of something being done,
the clack of a completed cycle.

I like the fairground thrill
of clothes spinning,
the vicarious excitement
of domestic life
possibly out of control—
blowhole in the sink,
Titanic in the hallway.

I like the taking out and untangling
the conundrum of wet clothes,
the thankful flap of a shirt or singlet
rescued from drowning.

I like the shaking, hanging and pegging out of clothes,
joining others who bow their heads
then stand with arms upraised
to hail the line
with clothes, flags, prayers or words,
a day's offering to the wind and sun.

Bio

Ross Donlon was born
He is a man,
a son, nephew, cousin and father.
He is a reader, writer and Reality Wrestler.
He has degrees in Dreaming,
First Class Honours in Fantasy,
post graduate work in Wondering.
His Master's research in to *Why?*
has recently been expanded and upgraded into a PhD incorporating
Why Not?
He has been highly commended for not entering poetry competitions,
both national and those of small country towns.
He has been forcibly rejected by some of the finest literary magazines in the country,
including *Northerly, Southerly, Easterly, Westerly* and *Meanjin.**
His published works include:
After which he self-published:
This latter was praised by Les Murray for its minimalism
and   use   of   space.
He reads his work
and is currently engaged in the major project
of being published
in *Northerly, Southerly, Easterly, Westerly* and *Meanjin.**

*Remembering that Frank Moorehouse said that 'Meanjin' is an indigenous term for 'material rejected by the *New Yorker.*'

BOOTLEGS

My Ship

After the composition by Kurt Weill

Dawn trims the horizon. Near a sheltered cove, ropes tighten as my ship
senses sunlight. Sails beat like a drum as I step on board my life, my ship.

Silver chevrons speed from the prow as the sun strikes. White triangles
haul in sky. Waves splash the echo of two words into the wake, *my ship*.

A young mariner morning, flushed with excitement, brushes canvas,
tips the mast red. Streamers foam gold in the wake of my ship.

Crests cut in a pattern of wings exhale the sea, breathe the waves
into shape shifters grooming miles into time beneath my ship.

Ripples shimmer sounds into sea-wrought poems and songs;
they fill the wind and drive the furrowing spine of my ship.

Evenings close the sun's gold door with a click.
Sea music clinks from the ruffled spire of my ship.

Glimmers of settlement fall away, dissolving like memory.
A lone lighthouse sweeps time and land away from my ship.

Clouds stream west, drain filigrees of days into years.
Cirrus fingers set a sky-compass north for my ship.

At night, a kaleidoscope of stars fractures the Milky Way.
Glittering like a merry-go-round, the cosmos orbits my ship.

Beyond north, cold holds fast to ropes and sails.
Frost mirrors reflect the icy course of my ship.

At the peak of the world, the sun skips earth like a fish.
Above, another ocean waits, sky-bound berth for my ship.

Some vessels pull against the incoming tide to eternity.
This sailor flies to destiny in the jagged kite of his ship.

Continental Drift

The children leave like continents
leaving Gondwana, the first continent.

The Old World splits like an atom,
becomes *Incognita*, the unknown continent.

Climate changes. Oceans rise,
drowning memories of a continent.

Evolution turns another way. Land
bridges dissolve, marooning a continent.

Where is landfall with so much land fallen?
Will a horizon ever return to this continent?

Where they were the coast is not clear.
I tell the history of a dying continent.

Bread

Bread is the best word in English when you want bread.
Just one syllable, honest as a full stop, serves for *bread*.

One letter begins and ends *bread* with a consonant crust.
Two round vowels hold the heart of hearth-made bread.

Flat as desert, moulded like hills or rucked like a range,
geography and culture make tasty ingredients for bread.

Rhyming with primals, like head, bed, wed and
dead, no tricks and twists perplex the ear when you hear *Bread*.

Yet this simple staple food was robbed by religion. Priests
turned dough into breasts, vulvas and penises. *Poor bread!*

So, when you eat the body of Christ at Communion be careful
of the bones. And *Did You Know* Bethlehem meant 'City of Bread'?

'The Staff of Life,' defined in 1638 as: a *staple or necessary food*,
is (in a French stick) a walking support when we shop for bread.

Ross's bread rises like him with the sun. Like him it's uneven, thick as a brick,
yet both taste good loved up with a cuppa. Ross writes honest bread.

Butter

Wið geswell, genim þas ylcan wyrte myllefolium mid buteran gecnucude.
Roughly, 'For a boil, take the yarrow plant mixed with butter.'
(This is the first recorded use of 'butter' in English.)

The Greek words *boutyron* joins *bous* (cow, ox) and *tyros* (cheese) to make our word for butter
Cow's Cheese might sound loony as a cow jumping over the moon, but that's the story of butter

What do you think of when you think of butter? I remember Nan buying a *Stick of Norco*,
something almost alive in the ice box like a delicious piece of sun. Or sin. *Ah butter.*

50's memories. No Butter Bloke but there was the Bread Man. Horse and cart parked, he gallo
upstairs to our bread box. We waited in our flat like brigands, ready to mug hot bread with bu

There we eschewed crust (later used to make curly snails) and dived into a wheat-warm womb
slathered gold. And with vegemite, honey or red jam we added bliss to the blessing of butter.

And so to sex. Has essence of cow cheese never occurred to you as you reached for the heights
Yet far beyond the pharmacy's packs waits the original lubricant of Eros. *Helloooo, butter!*

My friend's thing was shaving cream. He loved to brush love poems onto his lover's pelt.
Me, I dreamt of fun couplings with lashings of *Norco*, but could never wait for my butter...
to melt.

Knife

a word of uncertain origin

And origin is uncertain, perhaps, since we've been for so long with *Knife*.
How soon after we crawled did flint, shell and need take us to Knife?

Oldest tool. Oldest weapon. Hurting and helping. Which came first?
Protector or death-maker in peace and war - the checkered history of Knife.

Blade length varies with purpose, owner's age and gender. Culture curves,
straightens. Ornate or utilitarian, it wears the owner, heralds the bearer. *My Knife.*

Grandfather had his made in a railway workshop. Like him, roughhewn. Rough.
Rivets of cold steel. Handle not from bone, wood or plastic. Mystery of his Knife.

Never used. Never made to carve, cook or clean. It waited, sheathed inside him.
His kitchen throne room. His servants and lackeys. His joker. His hidden Knife.

His voice was a knife. Words slashed. Time can deepen a wound-cut memory.
Dream transforms pain into symbol and metaphor but the seed comes from Knife.

I retrieved it rusting in the past. What did it mean to me now? So many had died
other deaths. Cleaned and sharpened, its memory still glowed. And what is life to a knife?

The Horses

For Kristin Holst

Three twelve-year old girls have turned into horses,
but hold reins as they trot- to be riders and horses.

They canter in circles through the tall summer grass,
winding the spell that turns girls into horses.

And now there is song, a climbing helix of notes
a phoenix might sing to a troupe of passing horses.

So primal, this need to feel freer than humans can be,
to run faster, fly higher - beyond the self - to be horses.

In the park there are ramps where skateboards clattered
but the girls find work to make jumps for three horses.

Two take turns to lie still as water but the third props,
careful of her friends, before leaping; the mercy of horses.

Heads erect, their pony-tails catch the bobbing sun.
I watch from another time, as one should with horses.

origin of the species

For Caihong juji, a species of theropod dinosaur that lived 160 million years ago in Northern China. It was a duck sized animal which had iridescent plumage all over its head and chest.

you wake
to massed voices rippling
a curtain drawn back
on a shared past
and dreams
hauled to the surface
through a membrane of memory
sky callers
early talkers
first to wake
first to sing at light and us
kindred of earth and sky
when evolution made
one walk one fly

they thrill each morning
as the sun breaks
eons into sound
and you wonder
for a moment
what you are

Feathers

I have never seen a feather fall
but sometimes a patch of white
has caused me a morning's grief
seeing where a cat had struck.

First a wound grows in the grass,
then a downy pattern reveals
a gateway between time
where a life just disappeared.

When I was a boy, feathers meant war,
and I struck one in my cap to prove it,
or fletched feathers into the slit of an arrow
I sent wobbling towards another boy's heart.

Older, I offered feathers to my child,
intermediary between her and heaven.
Look, this came from a being that could fly,
living on earth with us but at home in the sky.

Innocent again, I find feathers on walks
left like a guide or reminder. Or swimming
in a nearby lake, I stroke past islands
of duck down, gone in a touch, spellbound.

Writing about feathers and my life with birds
I type incorrectly (but with prescience)
of my own feather self, *father*, a transient being
also hovering between this world and another.

Winter Poem

Air still as ice,
as many leaves on the ground
as in trees, all leeching
scarlet-autumn to winter-white.
When they die and drop,
gravity still demands a last, fluttering waltz,
so they spiral down,
the smallest of birds.

Two eastern rosellas playmate,
scarlet-blue on skeletal branches,
an aberration in the dark
(an 'aboration', I think darkly)
and transform the line of trees
into grieving angels.

Crow commands a neighbour's chimney,
legs braced, wings raised, dressed to kill,
The Bird in Black
chanting spells fit for apocalypse.

If this poem were a gothic tale
that family would be in a lot of trouble later tonight.
A shadow would rap an unpleasant pattern
on their claw-scratched door, and tomorrow morning
there'd be four pale leaves on the ghost bark birch
ready to fall.

Body Corporate

It's not as if there were documents signed
when I took possession. The understanding
between owner and me had to be open,
since both knew my dwelling would change.
   I've had no real complaints.
The foundations always had a yen to shift
and my preference for a lighthouse topped
with a view of the past, present and future
only got so far as rickety stairs to an attic,
two bay windows looking straight ahead.

Of course, it would be difficult for any tenant
to maintain the space as first occupied. To ask:
Nothing on the walls. No extensions was fanciful
and especially hard to comply with the latter,
since extensions happen of their own accord.

And how to complain to the eternal landlord
regarding any structural deterioration, notably
in private places, the bathroom, the bedroom,
since despite the wear of passing years,
wiring and plumbing remain: *Original. As supplied.*

I accept that the lease was binding
and, as it was a handshake deal,
my infant paw clasping the finger of God,
I respect the undertaking would last only
until one of us dies.

Piano Tuner

i.m. Edward George Lang (1896-1929)

This is a poem about the gaps in a life,
the what we don't know about someone
in their dash (-) between birth and death.

Sent back a cot case, he never returned
to Murrumburrah-Harden, the slap-dash
town on two hills, creek in-between.

Not even for his mother's funeral, they said
when the wattle and daub life killed her
after service on the Domestic Front.

He was raised in a hard stall, they said,
known around race tracks as *the runt,
the jockey* or *the rabbit shooter,* that's all,

so why wouldn't he get up and go,
take off when a parade and drums
thumped glory down Albury Street?

He'd *See the world. Roast Turkey,*
but ticks on a clipboard showed more.
The rabbits trained a marksman.

14th of April 1918. Mont de Merris
gallantry under fire wins the Military Medal -
'the other ranks' Military Cross.

Wounded but not enough, he's sent back
to the front. Shot in both knees. A boat
with crutches brings him home to no one.

But War, never ready to end with Peace,
follows the soldier like a jealous partner.
Their reunion in Tumut kills him.

Well known locally as a piano tuner, an obit
says off-hand. 100 years later, the odd phrase
tinkles curiously over gaps, hard to
understand.

From convict's grandson to Military Medal,
shooter, clerk and physician to pianos—facts
strike discordant notes as to the sum of the man.

In convalescence, he'd embroidered a rising sun.
Long gone now, it once seemed a feminine thing,
but nearest to his touch on a piano, that delicacy.

Mending Boots

My grandfather, country born and bred—
His old man was a bastard, a relative said,
could not chop wood, hit a nail in straight
nor turn a screw, without wrecking its head.

When his factory boots had gone to the pack
he'd squat on the floor, turn the boot on its back
like a recalcitrant child, then hammer the sole
'til a mishit blow blistered his temper black.

Then, *Damn the thing be buggered*, he'd blast.
(Other oaths tipped kids downstairs fast),
shocked neighbours into shutting doors
until Nan brought scones and tea, a repast

to soothe his temper. Then she'd cut and fit,
mouthful of tacks clamped like a bit,
kneeling before a lifetime's marriage,
mending and consoling - used to it.

Loving Pop

As his power waned
Pop became infamous
for breaking codes of family etiquette,
trudging past guests in the lounge
singlet yanked over his privates,
shaggy bum saying good night.
Enthroned in kitchen with a saucer of tea,
blowing it cool with bulging cheeks,
he could make climate change,
tides rushing over the rim.
A bad day at the races, made his temper
by Vulcan out of Mt. Olympus.
The women looked away
but I copied the only god I knew,
balancing my saucer on boy's fingers,
sailing bubbles across to the world to him.
War child of the widowed daughter,
he looked down at me
with something like sympathy
or perhaps he went back to a happier time
before the Great Depression's
banks and bookies
erased his place in the world.
I could sit in the eye of his cyclone
while he circled me with stories—
the bush and bushrangers, Jack Lang,
the famous deeds of racehorses,
(saviours of the working man)
especially the horse god, *Phar Lap*.

I learned from him some affection
is stranger than the tidal pull of mother love,
more like the crossword at the heart of his paper;
hard to get everything right across a lifetime
down to the number you happen to reach,
and how questions posed by love, especially
in families, can have more than one answer.

After

the kitchen awake	my bedroom woke
adults' quiet noise	to adults' quiet noise
a doorfull of light	and a door full of light
I stand in the frame	I stood in the frame
exposed in pyjamas	exposed
touched by cold	standing in cold
mum nan aunt uncle	they were all dressed at seven
all dressed at seven	my mum nan aunt uncle
cups and saucers ticking	cups and saucers ticking
women looking away	the women looked away
from a drum roll of silence	in a drum roll of silence
a ritual had begun	before initiation, disclosure
uncle Wid from Westmead	jowly red-faced uncle Wid
who beats his children,	who beat children
nods me to my room	nodded me before him
sits with me on my bed	sat with me on my bed
opens a seam in my head	then opened a seam in my head
mate, your grandfather's dead	*Mate, your grandfather has died*
I'll leave you now, he says.	*I'll leave you now*, he said and did
saving memory, all have left -	saving memory, all have now left -
the flat, Bland Street, Ashfield	family the flat Bland Street
Sydney, The 1950's, a family	Ashfield. Sydney, The 1950's
six other decades - all gone now	and six more decades—all have disappeared
through the same empty door	through the same empty door

Road Kill

Sunday morning on the Calder
two bodies rise with the crest.
One, foreground left, unattended,
the kangaroo's back turned away
in what looks like embarrassment,
or someone's attempt at courtesy.

On the opposite verge,
someone at the dead biker's chest
makes the bloated belly bobble and hop.
Momentarily, it seems like disrespect
and we all slow   eyes right
to see legs and arms splayed,
like something washed up
by the morning tide.

His mates wave like leather scarecrows
on a windless day, witnesses to a perfect time
for a ride into the almost unknown.
But still their Harleys spread like a threat -
that diamond torque - arc of black - broken chain.

One bike still on its side, wheels stopped
in a turn of roulette, I shock myself
wondering why I feel as much or more for the 'roo
that hopped through a copper morning
innocent as a penny, all grace and life intent,
only to be marked with the rough cross of road kill
and grieve thinking how its day will end,
where be thrown as landfill.

All or Nothing

After The Small Faces, All or Nothing *video, the 'undis-torted version', 1966)*

1.

Location for the song has The Small Faces
on a European tour, playing *All or Nothing*
on a freezing Paris night, hung braziers
blurring the scene with ghosting spotlights.

Edits have the studio track and images in sync
for what You Tube calls 'The Undistorted Version'
of their first hit, so shouts are unrecorded
phantoms, white shadow breaths on winter air.

Look-alikes with gamin cuts and elfin faces,
they've yet to ignore the camera, grinning
when they suss the lens riding on the mime,
thrashing unplugged guitars and a dead keyboard.

Steve Marriot, once Lionel Bart's Artful Dodger,
twitches dance steps, mod boots flicking snow,
calls in a voice raw as the grave, how love must be
All or Nothing. The band shouts silent agreement.

It's an eerie metaphor, the glide of flames
in and out of the video, remembering Marriot
died in a fire he began, burning with all
talent can give, reduced to the ash of nothing.

2.

I watch the clip compulsively, still distorted
by how it back tracks to the fate of us,
the shouted words of a minor sixties hit
roaring through us, two ghosts on fire.

Our quarrels soared back and forth
like dancers smashing up a kitchen,
our needing love to be all, terrified
it had burnt into nothing.

Fear quickly turns into tears then rage.
Grief roves its lens from one to other,
look-alikes with our hot faces, typical
of a man and woman of a certain age.

Pain edits each attempt at truth.
The past blurs fact into myth,
shadow breaths on winter air,
rarely in sync with what happened.

Facts disappear. We stretch for them,
churlish children reaching back for toys,
trying to understand how our end began
the night we saw the filming of a band

*Steve Marriott died at home in a fire lit by his cigarette

Warren Mathews

A boy called Warren Mathews
came to school at the end of the war
when some fathers never came home
at all, and others returned in pieces.

And after we'd sung and raised the flag,
Warren marched us into class
beating time away from the drum at his hip,
while our shadows marched like soldiers.
.

Some swung stick arms and legs
keeping in step behind his drum,
others stumbled half-submerged in sleep,
but each day I followed him, dreaming.

Warren knew about time. It took nothing
for him to stroke a drive, rake a forehand,
flush out a pass, score a goal and win
each game as though time wasn't there.

Always the best at recess and lunch
he was absent in class or disappeared
when Sir broke the rest of us into subject
and predicate, and turned time into tables.

The sweat on his face was a mask of gold,
a black fringe shielded his eyes like a visor
when I fought beside him in schoolyard battles,
like a page with his liege lord. Or father.

Now, I wonder if he returned to Avalon,
with a tale the bard could turn into song,
or grow old in a suburb, disguised as 'Dad',
blocking balls in a driveway, careful of windows?

Portrait of a Refugee

Uncle Stan was a refugee but I don't know if he fled or simply came
from Hungary after the '56 revolution.
But he was a *Ref,* or *Refo,* as we called them.
I was eleven. My father was dead from the war.
One day he and his friend picked up my mother and her sister on a Sydney tram.
Then he married Aunty Gloria and they lived in Fairlight.
We stopped using words like *Ref* and *Refo* then.
Uncle Stan and his friend liked to call themselves *Continentals.*
We delighted the *Continentals* when they bumped into our ways of thinking.
They drank *Rheingold* instead of beer and were superior to us in manners and
experience, we thought.
I never knew what Uncle Stan did before the war - but his family name meant
'soldier' and there was a photograph of him in a cavalry uniform, sleek as a lion.
He fought with the Germans during the war when he was in the Hungarian army.
He would shrug in a continental way when he told us facts like this.
It was confusing because Germans were us boys' enemies, even though the war was
over.
We were still fighting Huns and Japs, jumping out of trees crying,
'Bombs Over Germany!' or 'Bombs Over Tokyo!' as we fell onto Australia.
Uncle Stan told a joke about the devil running off when Satan heard that a car he'd
jumped on was travelling down the *Road to Pure Communism.*
He didn't like Communism and voted Liberal, since he was in business.
We were working people and always voted Labor. Pop worked on the railway.
I didn't understand it at all, why were different to each other.
Uncle Stan did not like *The Chews,* either.
He told jokes about Jews. They made me wince even though I didn't understand
about Jews any more than I did Communism.
Uncle Stan worked very hard, late hours and trained to be a chef in a Sydney
hospital.
Later he owned businesses and made and lost many fortunes.
He owned land around Surfers' Paradise when it was swamp and mosquitoes
but sold before it became marinas and high-rise.
He would get bored, waiting to sell for a big profit.
Aunty Glor became obsessed with housework and would starch sheets.
She developed a nervous tic and was always swallowing *Bex* powders.
Uncle Stan owned many pairs of shoes and would go to King Cross
and when came back he would joke about the *business girls* or *mattress workers* he'd
seen, laughing the words across the room to us.
He came back from The Cross like a prince, with arms full of cakes and cheese

as if from the other side of the world. We had never seen the like.

One cake had a layer of sour toffee of top that had to be cracked and crunched, to get to the layers of hazelnut cream and biscuit underneath.

Uncle Stan was a family man and took to Aunty Glor's parents, my Nan and Pop. He cooked meals for us wearing an apron in the kitchen of our tiny flat, turning out meals as though it was a race.

We had never seen a man do this before, a tea towel tucked in his belt.

Nan sat amazed as he flowed between the stove, sink and refrigerator, almost dancing in swoops with cream.

His hands were quick. Once, he grabbed my mother's breast when she was getting out of a car. She told me after he died.

He could catch flies with his hand. I saw him stalking, before snatching the fly then flicking the fly. while alive, into a spider's web.

He enjoyed watching the fly, smiling as the spider flickered across the web towards it.

Uncle Stan learned how to do this, he told me, when he was *in the camps*.

It was the boredom.

Once he bought buttons in two colours and he and I filed down an edge on each one

and we sat on the back steps of our flats to make two football teams.

We played on the laminex kitchen table and he always won but I loved him for making game he played in Budapest.

When he and my Aunty Glor used to fight he would call our family *peasants,* which we were. We never had money beyond pay day. No house. No car.

Everything we got was on Hire Purchase and Lay Buy.

He spoke good English but always said, 'So far as *me* is concerned' when he was being serious.

But no one corrected him because we loved him.

Uncle Stan used to say he was *a sexy man* and we knew there were other women when he went out at night—working shifts, playing bridge and having affairs.

He was irritated by laws, especially those concerning traffic lights and speed limits.

When his son was small he would have the boy lie on the back shelf next to the rear window and look out for *cop cars* as they ran red lights on the way to an early shift.

He paid many fines and liked to hunt, driving up into the bush to shoot anything he could kill..

Later he brought his parents to Australia, *Anna* and *Oppa*, who were pale and unwell

Anna worked with him in the kitchen, making *Langos*, deep fried pastries eaten with tomato soup. She worked hard, sweating over the saucepans.

I taught Anna English words, like *television aerial*, and we loved each other.

But Aunty Glor never liked Uncle Stan's mother and stopped her coming to her house because Anna *made mischief.*

There were two children, a boy and a girl.

Later Aunty Glor died of cancer. They were close at the end, despite the fights.

When he ate out and liked a meal, Uncle Stan would go into kitchens without notice

to congratulate the chef.

It was typical then that he invited himself to join a performance when a visiting troupe of Hungarian gypsies came to Gosford, where he was living.

He was dancing onstage with the gypsies that night when he had a heart attack and died.

It was reported that, 'He left a blonde in the audience,' but no one was surprised to hear that.

He would be a grandfather now.

Refuge / Refugee

We run from those with a mission to kill us faster than words can be wrought.
Refugee entered recorded English in 1685 as Huguenots fled from Catholic France.
But what word did we use before?
Were we merely 'other' - tribe, race, religion, colour?
Sentences created in conventions or social media spread safety nets of pity
or outrage, but fail to compete with the speed of failure.

Our word comes from the Latin *Refrigium*: Re—**back** + figure (**to flee**)
perhaps expressing the being in flight *from*, while longing to go back *to*—
as we fly from words that will change or ruin a way of being.
Listen.
our laggards are being over-run. Faith comes in the rustle of harness,

In an Antique Land

The synagogue in Marasesti Strada, Timișoara,
is enclosed by market stalls and swarming shoppers.
Its doors are high and wide, a solid brick structure,
secured with a band of stars at the height,
and crowned by a window with the Star of David.
Twin towers, with a *Moorish influence*, spiral dizzyingly
toward the sky, yet this is only of historical interest today
since the building isn't used for worship anymore;
the stone book of Torah wide open on the roof
like an offering or declaration, could be closed.

For the space is now used, we're told, for 'cultural events',
and today a rock festival poster with whirling symbols
of space and time, promoting, *The Popular and Unknown*,
only hint at irony.
So well preserved a structure shouldn't recall *Ozymandias*,
Shelley's sonnet destruction of a self-styled 'King of Kings',
but given the holocausts of the twentieth century,
the solid seeming walls still recall a 'colossal wreck'
and the phrase, 'nothing beside remains', still has meaning.

The First One

He is there, of course, for the first one, nursing
the old V Dub, flicking its indicators carefully
at each intersection on the safest way to hospital.

He works two jobs, proud if ends met. She
makes the best possible nest from little.
Both clutch his twenty minutes between shifts.

They'd walked right through the looking glass
of marriage. Seven months of life together later
shards still glow like jewels on the road back.

The birth takes hours of tears, holding hands
and hoping, future blank as hospital sheets,
personal charts hidden from them for now.

Love is there, intoxicating as parenthood,
and the child enters each of them as it enters
the world, red manikin bright with a power

so fierce the man thinks that father/mother
must be some hybrid, two-hearted creature
made from the need to keep on caring.

But the newborn's baptism is in mother blood,
father to one side, an acolyte, attendant being,
a soul apart.   Fathers know what I mean.

After the Election - On Rye Pier

After the painting, Rye Pier, *by John Baird*

With the sky thick as mud,
horizon steel edged, ship on its tightrope,
smoke from the stack smudging clouds,
the water at Rye flat as paste,
flowerets of spume and seaweed
regular as scattered cornflakes,
Rye Pier itself stark
in the afternoon as an abandoned shrine,
Tony Abbott looking on like a bemused pit bull terrier,
tail upright, head judiciously cocked,
the empty beach like Ava Gardner's
a good place to make a film about the end of the world
and with nothing to be gained but doubt
I dive into the election result and attempt a
somersault, pike and reverse twist
with the tide out.

Sunblock

For J.H.

As we dried off from the swim, she asked,
'Would you like me to rub your back with sunblock?'

But my first thought was that my freckled back
was as unreachable now as my speckled past.

What if she pressed a psychic button, released
a who knew what into the world? And *Sunblock*,

so redolent with metaphor. The word orbited
my quiet universe like a runaway asteroid.

Would the result be amusing or perplexing?
She might discover a *Terra Incognita* of me

with the dots joined up. My Rorschach blot?
(Human touch can trigger revelations, you know.)

And she *did* prise memories from my shoulders,
Lara Croft finding covenant-hidden springs,

finger nail surprising what I thought long lost.
Two blades quivered. Primaries flickered. I had wings.

Lemonicious*

*a *dwarf patio lemon tree*

Winter was hard,
the terra cotta tubs sentinel
as funeral urns in the courtyard.

But Spring unfurled early
in *Lemonicious*, the dwarf lemon.
Its white buds shone in purple lanterns,
a celebration life beside death,
while the other lemon, *Eureka*,
named for the ejaculation of success
(and subject of many transplants)
still lay dormant, flat lining
beneath five nursing leaves.
And I wonder if it's the absurdity
of being called *Lemonicious*
that provokes the modest variety to thrive
while its famous cousin stays fast asleep.

It reminds me of the twins born in the states,
Winner and *Loser.*
Loser played his name like an ace,
dealing life a full house.
Winner had no chips to spend from birth
Cursed with a name like *Eureka,*
he was flushed from the start.

Called *Lemonicious,*
he might have been president.

Being Puggle

After Lorraine le Plastrier's *wood carving, Platypus with Puggles and Nest*

The name for a young platypus is a platypus.
  Wikianswers.com

I was discovered covered in Latin.
Enlightenment scientists thought me a hoax,
others a joke God made when he was stoned.

First Nations had me a product of wayward duck
and rat—names numerous as eucalypts:
booraburra, mallangong, tambreet, dulaiwarrung...
The English explored me for signs of trickery
sewn by oriental stitchers—foreigners
trying to fool the rule of Britannia.

Forced to admit me to the study of fauna
Europeans gave me a suite of names,
a trail of words leading back to the Garden;
steropodon galmani begat *obduron insignis*
begat *platypus anatinus* begat *ornithorhynchus paradoxus*
begat *ornithorhynchus anatinus.*

'Platypus',
being already bagged by a beetle, shouldn't have stayed.
But did. Now it's a tag that won't go away.
Puggle jumped on me like a christening flea
with a mania for naming. So I'm also a soft toy, beagle-
pug and baby echidna all using the same moniker.

I can lap milk from pools on my mother's belly.
It's impossible, but I do it anyway
and laugh like Puck at all I see, thinking,
Oh, what fools these mortals be.

Vampire

For my daughter, Astrid

You always were a round, rubbery infant,
stuffed into jumpers and nappy pants,
bulging cheeks red with teething
big eyes shining at each new thing.
Babies are supposed to be wide-eyed, but you
woke ready to take the lid off every day
to pull the sun down to play, like a neighbour.

In the garden, each exploration seemed to end in scars,
as if your senses sent you to every compass point at once.
Yet no amount of cuts and stumbles
could stop each minute's tumble into life.
You even ate it.
earth dribbling down your mouth,
like blood.

Rose

For my granddaughter

Codes and letters line the scan
of you at seven weeks, six days.

Darker than a nightclub,
a semi sweep of light swings

across your mother's womb,
flickers on tucked up head and toes,

belly an equator, poles revolving
and turning on your own axis.

Girl Gulliver, floating gravity free
on a nine-month odyssey,

you orbit in time with a lifeline
firmly secured to the universe.

No wonder you seem to smile
from this one-person planet.

In a dark, wild world
pulsing with blood, you're held,

cradled in a half circle joined
like hands, like a rose opening.

Giant Steps

Like the assassination of J.F.K. six years earlier,
I remember where I was for the Apollo landing:

Trans Australia Airlines' Booking Hall.
Philip Street, Sydney. A screen flickers silent pics
above ticket clerks, baggage handlers and travellers.
Pedestrians come and go with lunchtime sandwiches.

Fifty years on and without being too droll,
I posit we all were making hazardous journeys
through space that day. Work. Home in peak.
The Relationship. One small step. One giant step.

More crowded than usual on ground floor T.A.A.
the show might have been to look at other aliens -
the Royals, a Grand Final parade, The Beatles.
The screen shone like an idol on a pole.

Already leached of all but subtle colours,
the moon turned black & white then ghost grey.
Two blobs with quivering aqualungs bobbed
inside a moonscape tank. Boys in Space.

Next, a tinfoil Stars and Stripes stood
at petty attention while America saluted.
A more pathetic act I never saw.
Question of scale - maybe more.

Later, Armstrong and Aldrin slow-hopped away
from no moon monsters. Golf on the moon.
The flag blew away when they blasted off,
leaving us with a mess of memory worms.

But Kennedy. That hurt, being human.
Brave flash of Jackie's pink dress on the black Caddy.
Death will do that. Oswald. Ruby. And loss of hope
before an abyss far deeper than outer space.

Walking on Green Cheese

Art begat Science.
Long before July 20, 1969
story, film and cartoon rockets
had already stuck pencil noses into the moon.
By 1958 Hannah and Barbera
rendered the Apollo mission unnecessary.
That year Tom Cat and Jerry Mouse flew to the moon, clean as a whistle,
completed a geological research project with speed and efficiency,
located and communicated with local inhabitants (tiny cat / giant mouse)
and safely returned while NASA was still asleep.

In the final 78 LP report, packaged by MGM and released to the public (in the same year)
Jerry Mouse proved conclusively that the moon was not made of green cheese
despite outward appearances to the contrary.
Using empirical research (he bit it, nearly breaking a tooth),
long-standing questions regarding the moon's geology were resolved.
Science trundled on. More than ten years later
Armstrong and Aldrin bounced about like balloon animals.
In the meantime, others bent their minds towards further reaches
of scientific research and threats to our existence from a galaxy far, far, away.

*__Tom and Jerry__ is an American slapstick cartoon comedy. Its original run of 114 episodes ran from 1940-1958 and it is still produced.

In Your Wake

Our never having met,
I only ever refer to you as *my father,*
yet sometimes wonder what I might have called you
in Louisville, Kentucky, your home, or in Sydney, mine.
Father has no currency in my class,
so words forever unused and unsaid—*Dad, Pappy, Bill*
taste like copper on my tongue.

Even now, what word to use on that continuum
where I follow seventy years later,
never to meet, nor pass by it seems,
always in the slipstream of your spell in light,
ever in the wake of that last voyage,
and ironic end in *The Ferry Hotel,*
where you waited to sail or die.

My ship ever *in the wake,*
so self-consciously poetic
I smile to think of the recurring symbol
I've carried like DNA from kindergarten locker
(circle sun / trim white sailing boat / rippling sea)
into the abyss of tonight.

Writing 'another ship poem',
pitching into a sea of stars,
hauling and trimming the sail of poetry,
I search from the bow for a man ghostly and god-like
as the Flying Dutchman,
and I wonder if in eternity, should there be a landfall there
I will see you waiting with a name for me
I can find some way to return.

The Man with a Bucket

Killcare, N.S.W. 1944

She tells the story of when he went shopping with a bucket,
walking along their honeymoon beach, the soldier with a bucket.

She's cut the legs of his army fatigues to make swim shorts
so he paddles in surf, list in his pocket snug next to the bucket.

Their honeymoon home is a shack sheltered in sand hills
and at night the moon shines back brimful from a silver bucket.

The beach near Sydney is called *Killcare* but they are care-less
as she sends him away, splash-happy, to shop with a bucket.

It's true, he becomes a mirage in the heat waving back,
or quite disappears in surf haze, a ghost clutching a bucket.

But after five days the world appeared. Dressed in its uniform
he marched to the dock, carrying kit instead of a bucket.

Like a couple in Eden, my parents, in their honeymoon idyll,
on leave from time, innocent as apples brought in a bucket.

The Metaphor-Boat

I come to a village in Norway every year
and each time see a fishing boat moored there
roped between two green lines, bow to stern,
a tightrope craft hung on water, unable to turn,
go forward or reverse, subject to weather and tides.
It's rotting, above and below the waterline.
The mast, broken in half, now lashed to the bow,
might speak of working life, but it also shows
a gesture to antiquity, as though someone yet
might balance on the prow, hauling a spinnaker
to let it fly off the wind on a reaching course,
a man to envy, brave and full of guile, like Odysseus.
The hull was blue, is now grey or patched white
like the cabin, whose unpainted door looks bright
in contrast. Two small windows squint towards aft
like fashionable retro specs (cool, rectangular, daft).
The covered hold is tightly lashed. Tonnes of mackerel
have quivered there ice-bound from a good day's catch.

And the boat also teems for me, but with metaphor,
an insight provided into the years I've roamed.
For a man, aging now like a stubborn boat,
who's seen off storms and time (but still afloat),
what to choose to sail this craft into the world
crewed by quick witted figures of speech. Which words?

For preference, I'll like to be like Puck - ever changing.
So sometimes those backward-looking eyes I have to be,
bleary with the past, consumed by the dreaming wake,
some days the mast, broken and lashed - outdated.
The sturdy hull? It stays afloat, plugged and repainted,
rough and tough, its lines still look elegant (in reflection).

Ships fascinate me. Born landlocked in an upstairs flat
suspended between earth and sky, I watched craft
sail through moons and stars, felt the drift of nightly tides,
the bobbing calm, the roll and tuck of a wild ride,
the longing to sail for home and always stay.
Naming boat parts gives me a metaphor-a-day,
And tonight, I'll be spinnaker that frees this noble wreck.
Braced on the prow, I'll leave this world for the next.

The Rain in Garana

The rain knows about the jazz festival.
That's why it comes every summer.
Clouds displace the sun early as Thursday
and rise from Timișoara through Resita
because rain likes the best seats in the house.

Musicians still play, artists still create,
fans still sit under plastic, eating *langos,*
the salty pastries that love good times.
The rain thinks it provides accompaniment
to music & beer for four whole days.

Each night, it be-bops or blows cool
with the squally wind, keeping time
across the hills, sharing its riff
with wolves who watch stars dissolve.
.

At last the rain takes a long solo on the roof,
making tempo faster than Art Blakey,
then ending in a one note tear drop.
Finally, with no more than brush strokes,
it lifts the last band into the night
and they all bring down the house.

To the Viewer

After the painting, Self Portrait, *by Ian Armstrong, 1948*

I know why you are looking at me,
my dark eyebrows raised,
shirt unbuttoned enough
to show a shadow of hair,
hair tousled as if you've
just run your hands through it,
leaving my cheeks blazing.

And although my ears still tingle
at what you suggest—and my mouth
is half-open, as if to say no (or yes),
my eyes appraise you from some seventy years ago
which suddenly (and sadly) seems too long
to find out what we'd like to know.

Reconciliation

After the painting, Reconciliation, *by Tom Roberts*

The title of this painting
could be embraced by inverted commas,
since the 'reconciliation' of the young man and woman
seems some way off.

She's still dressed from last night,
a ball where the tiff took place,
before she walked into the morning.
Her eyes still look starry,
not looking at him,
but at the past, perhaps,
or into another future.

He's coming searching.
His boots and leggings
show he went home, changed, came riding back.
Consider the symbolism:
an overgrown path,
awkward for a woman in a ball gown,
leads back to a solitary horse.
How far has she already come?

And they're stalled inside a maze of trees,
still inside a kind of dance,
like last night's *Pride of Erin*.
His eyes are willing her to look,
but she avoids him, unconvinced.
His right hand holds her shoulder,
trying to make her turn,
but she won't be moved.

Lady from the Lake

Some way after Keats

He saw her rise from the evening
and stand in her own reflection
raising her arm to show him something,
a shell perhaps, that glittered in her hand
before she dived into herself again.
And, of course, he should have known,
should have remembered her name,
one of those who come and go lightly
shy of the sun—*a belle dame.*
But when she walked by,
water streaming like chains,
her first words a spell,
he stayed with her til the slit of dawn
before she left him in hell -
and returned to the past,
always her home, leaving him
on a hillside, pale and loitering,
waiting for her and the dark to come,
alone.

Let's Call This

Title after the composition by Thelonious Monk

Come live with me and be my love
and let's say this is it,
what scientists call the chemical hit
that puts two people together,
most needs met,
our cups half-full, or full enough
for everyone to get wet.
For we've passed every test modern love requires,
opening credits rolling through the cabfight in the rain,
the storyboard scenes of trial and bliss,
the embers that became flames.

Who cares if the ex from the dead showed up
when garlic and crucifix were nowhere around,
or when a wide-eyed child arrived one day
insisting they were somebody's.
Or when the friend from hell
threw up the past all over the present
and Death itself scanned a page
before a life fell out like a bookmark.

Let's say after all that we made it, it was fate,
and high above the mass dysfunction
of twenty-first century life,
our sun set over everything,
the moon shot up like popped corn,
an all-star sky twinkled,
we kissed
and rockets spelt our names in lights
above the Empire State.

Geraniums

Geraniums grow where light is indifferent.
They deck derelict homes in derelict suburbs,
colour splattered rather than applied
green camouflage dotted with flowers.

Never the first bloom to show a child,
that surprise is reserved for perfumery -
roses, violets, the pansy's summer face
a shy dragon to snap an infant's nose.

More likely we crawl or stumble by ourselves
into the geraniums' house of knobbly knees,
dull foliage and buds like the caps of fairies.
Secrets take warmth and time to come forth.

Like Baba Yagi's scary, alluring cottage
on chook legs, we sense ancient mysteries
in the musky leaves and crisp petals
darkening the geranium's forest floor.

So they don't feature in florists' displays
where candy bright shouts, elegance bends
reserved and subtle on a lambent stem
and exotics seduce from another culture.

Who sends their lover geraniums,
or fills an envelope with geranium petals
for her to open, the way we do roses,
spilling heart-deep on her kitchen floor?

But geraniums won't rake for blood,
as roses do, nor fade with waking,
petals falling like an autumn path
waiting to be swept away.

So I will give my lover geraniums,
simple but renewing in tiny suns,
filling gaps in her house and garden
with their endurance.

The Sex

My friend
speaks of sex, as though it were a pet
parrot perhaps, gardening folly, travel plan,
virus, unusual plant, something you get in your head
instead of in bed.

'How's the sex?' she'll ask,
and I think Colosseum, Eiffel tower, Leaning Tower of Pisa,
Jonathon apple glowing in a poison tree,
cut glass bowl with trifle and whipped cream,
bustling dragon with umbrella wings,
tango on a beach in Rio, phosphorescence streaming.

But if she'd asked today, I'd have said,
'Like the scene in the reservoir where I swam
this evening. As the light fell away, a swallow's
fluttering home was barely reflected in the water,
as though neither of us was really there.'

Titanic

Or lines written after seeing an inflatable Titanic used as a
children's slippery slide at Apollo Bay.

We all loved Princess Di. After her death
we lined her kingdom and lowered the flag
but the fairy tale ended next morning at work
when The Fool arrived with his funeral gag.
The boy's suicide is tragic forever (for a while),
until someone found a joke inside the sorrow.
Some winced but someone had to smile. We call it
processing. Tsunamis in Aceh are surfing contests
on the morrow; Jesus drops his cross on the parade;
holocaust clothes and brands become fashion statements
in Japan; cartoons create small wars. So, remember,
when your private iceberg floats towards you
and it looks like this is it, check out the streamers
and gang of laughing funsters, waving from its icy tip.

(On) About Suffering

'About suffering, they were never wrong, the Old Masters.'
W.H. Auden, Musée des Beaux Arts.

In the cool schools of the north, maybe so.
Can't you hear the 'peasant' Breughel?
Lad falls from sky. Man ploughs, sees now't,
Lad drowns. Sun shines. Ship sails on t' port.
In the south, Papal edict and convention decreed grace,
not grief. By the time nails crunched in, the victim's face
was in another place. The eyes roll and there's a half-smile
and the body seeps. Cherubs grin from bubbling clouds
while relatives weep. Sebastian's chest is riddled with darts
but Sebastian has gone. Ecstasy relieves his mouth, the smart
of wounds dulled by the deepest drug of all; religion
casts its pall over what it really means to be human.
Young makers have more chance to get suffering right
in dispatches from our poor world at seven every night.

Cardinal Paleotti, for example, in a treatise on religious art, *Discorso in torno
alle immagini sacre e profane (*1582), well known in Rome, 'believed that art
should be traditional and conservative that naturalism should be tempered
by classicism and should not shock or disrupt'. \Helen Langdon.
Caravaggio A Life.

the origin of the poem

when I see my brain
on the surgeon's screen
I see headlights of poems
scorching word circuits
hurdling prose clots
skimming writer's blocks
punctuating pit stops
and when the eye sockets beam
twin laser rays of emerald green
and the jaw cracks open its checkered-tooth grin
that's a sure sign
a poem is nearing the line

Netball in Newlyn

For my daughter, Eithne

Newlyn is quiet,
only shadows play in the park.
Then netball lights flicker,
kick on. Drills start
as stars start to connect
above a turquoise court,
tiny, turquoise planet,
gold rings at each end.
Light bulbs grow worlds
freckled with moths.
Girls run and shout,
arms outstretched.
Sneakers squeak.
A mum calls out instructions.
And I'm glad there's netball in Newlyn,
a blink-and-you-missed-it place.
whose lights dissolve as you climb the hill.
It gives me heart to see them train,
to run and pass almost by instinct.
It reminds me how we make and do
in Newlyn, or New York, or anywhere
someone tries to do something
more than survive a night and day.
It's why I write - to move space, imagine,
make order of emotion, thought, action,
try to score a goal.

After Yorick

All bards become Yorick,
half-sunk skulls in mud.
(Poets' lives are mostly short.)

Wit or rhymester, the cohort
driven by word-flood
is easily winged, then caught

on the road less travelled,
sport in motley for ironic gods.
Still. When Orpheus

calls fools to word riot
I follow. Post -Mods
can scoff. I'll stalk

this life, make report.
Be it long or short
I'll stay the course.

At the Poetry Reading

I wish to advise that the following poems
are rated *M* for a mature audience.
They contain violence, nudity, a sex scene
and strong use of language.
Sixty-nine per cent of the content has been classified as emotional, possibly nostalgic.
This may cause drowsiness in some listeners and increase the effects of alcohol.
If so affected, do not drive a motor vehicle or operate heavy machinery.
If you are pregnant or hoping to conceive, don't listen.
I hope you enjoy the poems,
even that lights flicker on in your cortex
but in the unlikely event of an emergency
please brace yourself by holding on tightly to a person next to you.
(You may wish to negotiate a partner now, since a refusal later may offend.)
Oxygen masks will fall from the ceiling.
Please see to yourself before attending to children or the infirm.
If it is necessary to abandon a poem entirely, listen for the conveniently placed line breaks
and punctuation marks until you hear the last full stop.
Exit by sliding beneath the poem (*Mind the Gap*) and fall to the floor.
Assume a foetal position and wait for further assistance.
Warning: Please ensure you take all belongings with you.
Any ideas left unattended may be taken away and plagiarised.

At the (Much Wenlock) Poetry Festival

(After Breughel)

For Anna Dreda

As though gravity had suddenly become horizontal
patrons run from the town square,
drawn by the magnet of poetry.
Arms point, faces gawk, legs buck
as they try to run in different directions.

A woman abandons her corset of couplets;
a man fears for his postmodern codpiece;
girls and boys laugh at the upturned town
as they gaze through words to new worlds.

Wenlock Books strains at its spine,
Owner, Anna, is multi-armed deity, books waving in each hand.
Money clutchers quiver with reader fever;
the moon jumps over a cow;
Christopher Robin jumps out of the closet;
Poet Laureates dance with Parrot Lorikeets;
owls and pussycats busk with the Jumblies;
barrels of ballads roll down to pubs
already awash with sonnets.

Then Titania and Oberon agree on the weather for just three days
while Puck trails stars over the Much that is Wenlock.

OUT TAKES

Fables for Our Time 1: The Sheep and the Asteroid

Once upon a time,
a stranger heard a flock of sheep blaring
so loudly he had to stop the car and look.
The sheep were packed into a life-preserver circle,
trying to squeeze through an existential gap to Nowhere.
Lambs skittered and hopped over waves of grass

The watcher searched for a cause for this effect.
Was it the gate-keeper farmer big as god? God's border collie?
But the paddock seemed empty of any explanation
except for sheep being silly.

Then, missing until now as an undiscovered star,
a head appeared, red line skimming at the white circle.
It drove through grass, dorsal ears and grinning mask
slicing through waves with the speed of something
whose adrenalin kicked in on annihilation.

From the stranger's perspective, parked just across the road,
and looking into a universe strung with barbed wire,
the fox was like a Code Red asteroid careering towards Earth,
like the rock that brought an end to the dozy dinosaurs.
But this time the asteroid recalibrated to wreck a world some other time.
And the fox, inexplicably, stopped before the door to Infinity.
It ran bobbing back and lay panting beneath a summer tree
to count the sheep it didn't eat, before it fell asleep, sweet as a fable.

Moral: Don't count your sheep before they're extinct

Fables for Our Time 2 : The Trials of Sheep Dog

She tells the girlhood story of the orphan lamb
she loved and raised on the bottle on their farm
and I wonder if there's a lesson for us in this.

As her teenage self grows maternal, the baby-like
pet's eyes dream-like, the sticky, milky fleece
I sense an affecting story building in this.

The lamb so docile in the house, sleeping with dogs,
content with the family, tv and a pack of kelpies
I see a heart-warming metaphor coming from this.

But as time grows, she grows, the lamb too but—
alas into a ram, still so dog-like they call him *Dog,*
so familial, I warm to the steady devotion in this.

Yet while lambs might live in houses, rams cannot,
since rams like to ram - legs, doors, grandma,
I feel a sobering question emerging from this.

First day interned in a paddock Dog eschews the ewes,
then breaks his back leg chasing a tabby cat up a gum tree,
a surreal if comic tragedy surprising in this.

First time for everything, the vet makes a cast for the ram
hobbling pirate-like in a tilting sheep paddock, so poignant,
I hope a cheerful moral or metaphor might still come from this

Cast off but still outcast *Dog,* greets the missus' returning car
by ramming her door shut, then the other doors and boot
and I have a sense of foreboding looming over the sheep called *Dog.*

Marooned in her purple Gemini, Mum phones Pa, but his mobile is
silent while *Dog* looks for more vehicles to ram, and I imagine
Nietzsche, Jung and Freud debating with Plato and Epicurus as to what
wise conclusion might be drawn from such an unexpected pass.

Sunday dinner in the country is a time of calm,
baked meat and vegetables fresh from the farm.
Talk subdued, apart from courtesies, *Pass the ram.*

Moral: Self-awareness is the sheep-dip on the way to Enlightenment

Fables for Our Time 3: Sammy the Sheep

Thing is, we lived in a top floor redbrick two up/two down. Sheep
might bleat from radio serials but we knew nothing about real sheep.

Rhymes from Bo Peep could gambol from woolly blankets of sleep
but shepherds' crooks were more at home in books to us, not sheep.

Our world was blocks with bitumen roads and tar bubbling in the street
but right next door was the universe of a biblical beast - Sam the sheep.

Flat-life is unearthly, innocent. We called the neighbour's oak *an acorn tree*,
cicadas *locusts*. The keeper of both oak and locusts was Sam the sheep.

No cartoon lion was more fierce as Sam tore and crunched tender leaves,
bullied grass and bailed up the acorn tree where a boy hid, scared of sheep.

Tennis balls sent errant past our laundry wall were ruled completely
Over the Fence and Out, policed to sleep by Sam the Guardian Sheep.

But one mysterious Sunday Sam disappeared. Tennis balls were retrieved
in bucket loads from his demesne, religious relics from the god of sheep.

On Monday morning a shining ghost rose in the paddock, white as a sheet.
Clipped and glittering, Sam had transitioned into Samantha Sheep.

Lazy Catholics, we knew nothing of theology. Mass was *hocus pocus and
who hic hoc?* But I'd seen the Lamb of God, and knew it was Sam the Sheep.

Moral: A ewe in ram's clothing is still a sheep

BONUS TRACK

After the Fall

Sunday passed blithely by
and the world didn't quite end
as I mimicked a table
in the town gutter.
Nor did Heaven look on and laugh
while I was down and out,
no angels frolicked and jeered,
nor did fiends leer and point
down to flames as I kept falling.

But the road hurt when hands hit
and knees which have suffered long enough on this trip
stopped suddenly with cuts to match
with four pads, four pink flags of embarrassment.

The spilled shopping suddenly exposed
a life less measured in coffee spoons
than that Ross Donlon's was measured as:
one packet of dried yeast, six green pears, one school pak 750 g of bananas,
one bottle of Gold & Black sparkling mineral water.

Harder getting back up than I thought
(think querulous kangaroo rising long-eared,
planet-eyed looking at a Brave New World from a different angle).
The bubble in my spirit-level dipped out of sight as the horizon tilted
and I rolled along the road confused enough to mix up my mythologies,
Lethe lapping around the bend in Hargraves Street,
the one-eyed ferryman upside down on the Tree-of-Should-Have-Known-Better on Mostyn,
a Ragnarok moment in Castlemaine, Australia,
10.45 am, February 27, 2019,
lucky numbers saved up for a Tatts lotto ticket on Monday.
Then the sun zoomed in for a close-up dialling 37° C .of midsummer heat reporting
No Relief in Sight
                    and a kind woman calling,
 'Are you all right, sir?'

Afterword

For the Record contains my earliest published *Bulletin* poems, written when I was at school or in my teens on Samarai, PNG, as well as those from the last 20 years after I became active again. The ratio is about 50:50. The title attests both to my love of music and that my first-heard poems were lyrics from Tin Pan Alley. I love the word play, romance, darkness and humour of popular music.

I wonder also whether having the poems presented as 'tracks' like song lyrics, will affect the way they are received. Judith Rodriguez, a mentor, once said to me, 'Ross, some of your poems are frankly popular,' but I thought she was paying me a compliment, rather than giving me a warning. The final section of my first full-length book was called, 'Frankly Popular,' as a warm acknowledgement to her.

Judith also advocated that poetry be about 'total experience,' and there is a wide range of feeling underpinning my poems, from the very dark to the light and silly. Poems set in different parts of the world follow my travels. For me, form is determined by the subject of the poem, and there are a number of forms here.

So, apart from my Juvenilia in 'Rarities', the tongue-in-cheek 'Classics' are merely the stronger poems from early books, while 'Bootlegs' are those which have so far appeared only in anthologies, journals or nowhere. 'Out Takes' contains three poems called, *Fables for Our Time*, the title lifted directly from James Thurber. I'm fond of their nonsense. At 75, nearly 60 years on from 'August', I have bookended the work here with two poems about death, both comic.

It's been very interesting and illuminating structuring *For the Record*. It has enabled me to see more clearly what I do and what I have done.

Notes

1. Note on the *Bulletin* poems in Rarities:

The Bulletin's Literature Editor, Charles Higham, wrote in a review of the year, 1965 of 'some young poets in or just out of their teens who augur well for a more inventive Australian future…(including)…Ross Donlon, who, I believe, also has an exciting future.'

My next poems were published thirty-three years later.

Acknowledgements

Some of these poems have appeared in: *The Australian; The Bulletin; The Canberra Times; Crannog* (Ire.) *Cordite; European English Messenger* (Rom.); *Gitanjali & Beyond* (U.K.); *Meanjin; Plumwood Mountain; Poetry Ireland Review* (Ire.) *Quadrant; Salt-lick Quarterly; Skylight 47* (Ire.) Southerly; *THE SHOp* (Ire); *Westerly,The Arvon International Poetry Anthology 2011.* (U.K.) *Best Australian Poems 2014; Blue Dog; Contemporary Australian Poetry; Giant Steps; A Guide to Sydney Rivers; Kickers & Knockers; Much Wenlock Festival Anthology 2012 & 2014* (U.K.); *Poems for All Occasions; To End All Wars; This House, My Body; Writing to the Wire, Awakening—*poems from the collection of the Castlemaine Art Gallery; *Shh & other love poemsThe Blue Dressing Gown & other poems; Lucidity; Light Travelling; My Ship; Tightrope Horizon.*

Body Corporate was commissioned in 2018 as part of the show, This House, My body, a multimedia installation by Rachael Guy and Leonie Van Eyk.

The Blue Dressing Gown won the Much Wenlock Poetry Festival Prize (part of The Arvon International competition U.K.) judge, Carol Ann Duffy

Midsummer Night won the Melbourne Poets' Union International Poetry Competition—judge, Lisa Gorton

Thanks to the workshop group of Nathan Curnow, Ross Gillett, Anne Gleeson & Lorraine McGuigan who have seen some of these poems in transit and to Andy Jackson, and Rachael Wenona Guy.

About the author

Born in Ashfield, Sydney, Ross Donlon now lives in Castlemaine, Victoria, where he has convened literary events for over ten years. He has written four full length books of poetry, numerous chapbooks and won two international poetry competitions. Widely published in Australia and Ireland, he has read his poems extensively at home but also in many parts of Europe, including festivals in England and Ireland and other readings in Romania, Poland and Norway. He collaborates with Norwegian musician, Bjorn Otto Wallevik, as a lyricist and director of music videos, and is currently collaborating with musician Jeremy Challender on performance projects. Poems about his father, a WW 2 U.S. serviceman from The Blue Dressing Gown were a program on Poetica, a national radio program in Australia. He is publisher of Mark Time Books.